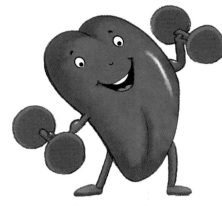

WHAT

MAKES MY HEART GO 'LUB-DUB'?

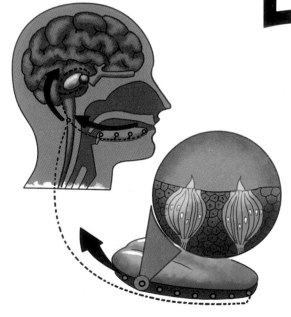

Om
KIDZ

An imprint of Om Books International

Contents

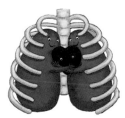

What makes my fingerprints special?

Press your finger onto an inkpad and then to a piece of paper. You will see a print of the lines and ridges on your finger—that's your fingerprint. Each fingerprint is unique. This means that no one else in the world has the exact same set of lines that you have on your fingers. Not even identical twins!

Find out

Why do we have wrinkles on the back of our fingers?

Pocket fact

You need 34 muscles to move your fingers and thumb: 17 on the palm and 18 on the forearm.

What makes my foot go to sleep?

Blame your nerves for this! When you sit on your foot, you temporarily compress the nerves. These nerves are then unable to send messages back to the brain normally, and so for the moment you don't feel anything. It's as if your brain is saying "Hello", but your foot does not reply.

What makes me feel dizzy when I spin?

Your inner ears have fluid inside them. When you spin around, the fluid inside the ears moves too. Even when you stop, the fluid continues to move for a while, bends tiny hair and sends a signal to your brain. This makes you feel like you are spinning backward. We call that "feeling dizzy".

Pocket fact

Your ear has three bones. These are so small that they can be placed together on a penny. They are the stapes, malleus and incus.

What does my outer ear do?

Your outer ear is called the pinna or auricle. The outer ear's job is to collect sounds and channel them through the ear canal towards the middle ear so that you can hear various sounds.

Find out

Why is ear wax important?

> **What makes my nose run?**

There is a sticky substance in your nose called mucus. Your nose runs when you catch a cold or flu. This mucus keeps the germs out of your lungs and the rest of the body.

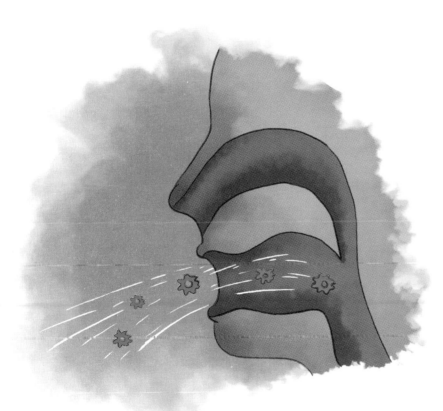

What makes me cough?

You cough because of excess mucus or when you inhale irritants that are present in the air. These irritants lie on the surface of your respiratory tract and the body tries to push them out in the form of cough. Coughing helps to clear the throat.

Pocket fact

A 12-year-old girl from UK, Donna Griffiths, holds the world record for the longest sneezing bout. She began sneezing on 13 January 1981 and kept sneezing for 978 days!

Find out

Some people have a very strong sense of smell. What is this called?

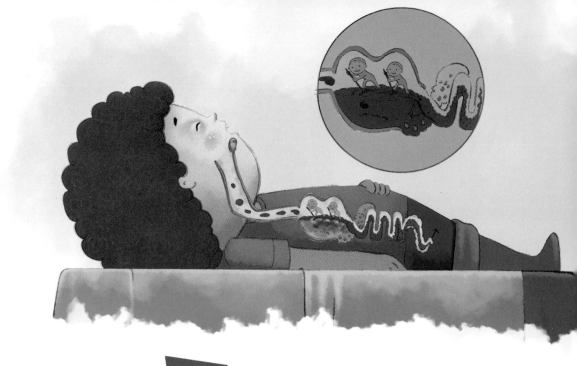

What does my tongue do when I sleep?

Your tongue never rests even after talking, swallowing, tasting, and germ-fighting all day long. When you fall asleep, your tongue is busy pushing saliva into the throat to be swallowed. If it doesn't do that, you would be drooling all over your pillows!

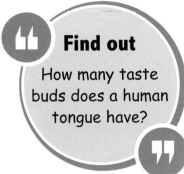

Find out

How many taste buds does a human tongue have?

Pocket fact

The tongue is the only muscle in your body that works without any support from the skeleton. This is known as muscular hydrostat.

What helps my tongue taste food?

The taste buds on your tongue let you know if the things you eat are sweet, salty, sour, or bitter. Taste buds have tiny bumps (papillae) and sensitive, microscopic hair called microvilli. These hair send messages to the brain about how something tastes.

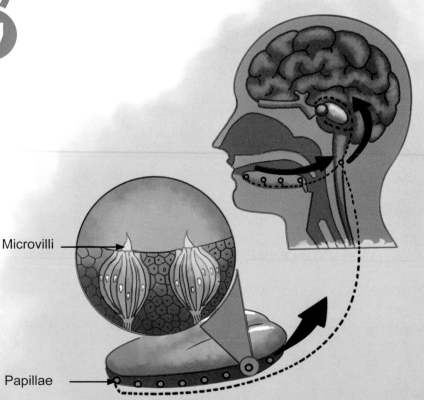

Microvilli

Papillae

What is cavity?

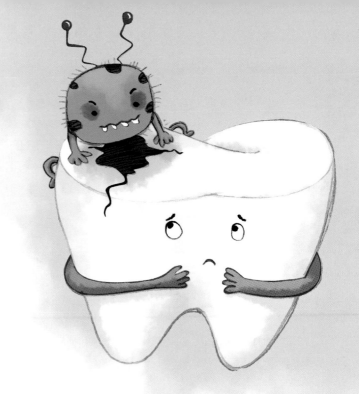

A cavity is a hole in the tooth caused due to decay or breakdown of the tooth. You get cavities because of a sticky substance (plaque) that carries germs. The bacteria in your mouth make acids and when plaque clings to your teeth, the acids corrode the tooth enamel.

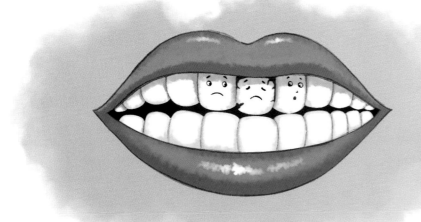

 Pocket fact

Oh I have Odontalgia! The scientific term used to describe toothache is 'Odontalgia'.

What makes my lips pink?

The skin on your lips has only three to six layers of cells compared to the 16 layers of skin covering other parts of the body. This makes the skin on your lip almost transparent. Your lips appear red or pink because of the blood capillaries that lie under this transparent surface of your lips.

Find out

Can your lips sweat?

What helps my eyes see different colours?

Your eyes have small cones that sense colour. Cones sense shades of red, green, or blue colour. Together, these cones can sense combinations of light that enable our eyes to see millions of colours.

Retina

Rods

Cones

Cone Cells

Rod Cell

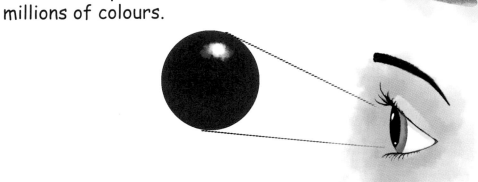

Lacrimal Duct

Lacrimal Glands

Lacrimal Ducts

Nasolacrimal Duct

Pocket fact

A human eye can see one million colours. It also has the extraordinary ability to distinguish different shades of the same colour.

Find out

Why do different people have different eye colour?

What's the special bathing system for my eyes?

Tears bathe your eyes! There are special glands called lacrimal glands, above the outer corner of each eye where tears are produced. Every time you blink, tears come out of the upper eyelid. Tears help to wash away germs, dust and other particles that can harm your eyes. Tears also keep your eyes from getting dry.

What makes scabs over my wound?

Your skin makes collagen—a tough, white protein fibre that acts like a bridge and reconnects the broken tissues. As part of the healing process, a dry, temporary crust covers the wound. This crust is called a scab. The scab protects the wound while the damaged skin underneath heals.

Find out

Where is the thinnest layer of skin on your body?

Pocket fact

Deep down in your skin, there are touch receptors called Ruffini Endings. They are sensitive to being stretched or squeezed, and they also respond to changes in temperature.

What gives me goosebumps?

When you feel cold or are scared, your body releases a chemical called adrenalin. This causes the little muscles at the base of each hair to contract and stand up. When this happens, your body creates an insulating layer and keeps your body warm. Goosebumps are just your body's way to make sure that you keep warm in the cold weather!

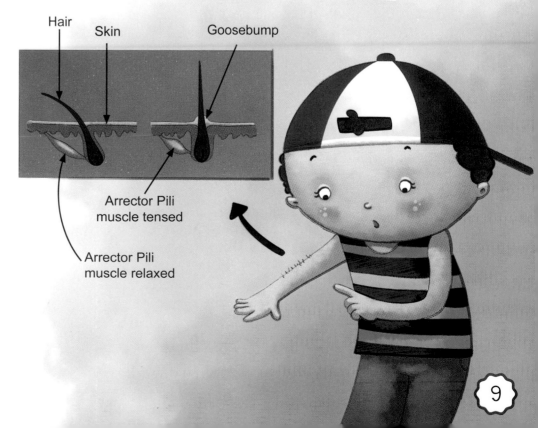

Hair   Skin   Goosebump

Arrector Pili muscle tensed

Arrector Pili muscle relaxed

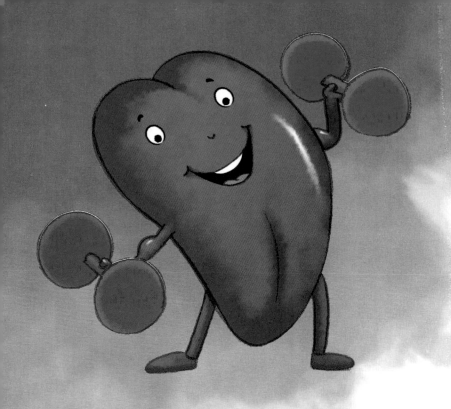

What is the strongest muscle in my body?

It twists, turns, bends and helps you talk! It's your tongue! When it comes to doing different kinds of work, your tongue is probably the strongest muscle in your body. It is made up of many groups of muscles that run in different directions to carry out all the tasks—talk, swallow, taste, etc.

Find out

There are different types of muscles in your body. But what are heart muscles called?

Pocket fact

Muscles get most of their energy from glucose. Glucose is made from carbohydrates such as sucrose (from sugar), lactose (from milk) or fructose (from fruits).

What makes my muscles cramp?

Your muscles cramp when they lock up, and you feel pain. This happens when one or more of your muscles contract and do not relax again (this is called a spasm). Exercising for too long, sweating and not drinking enough water can lead to a muscle cramp.

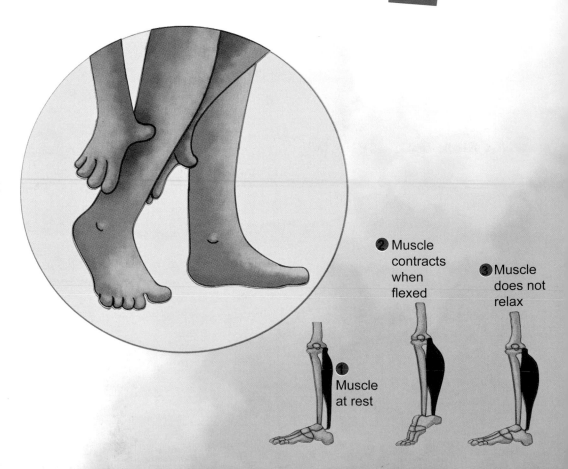

❷ Muscle contracts when flexed

❸ Muscle does not relax

❶ Muscle at rest

What are my bones made of?

Bones are made up of calcium, blood vessels and marrow. Around 70 percent of the bones in your body are made of calcium. The bone is hard, smooth and solid outside, and porous and spongy inside. A bone also has room for blood vessels which makes our bones slightly bendable. At the centre of bones is a softer substance called the marrow.

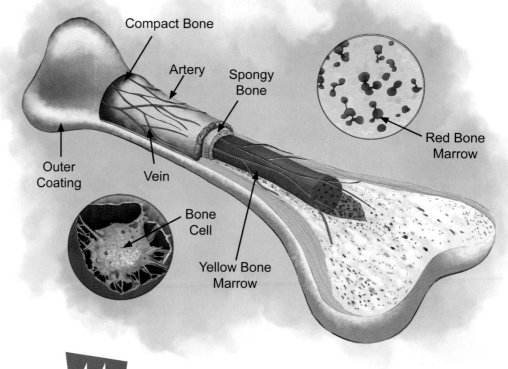

Compact Bone

Artery

Spongy Bone

Red Bone Marrow

Outer Coating

Vein

Bone Cell

Yellow Bone Marrow

Find out

How many bones does a baby have? What happens to the bones as it grows?

Pocket fact

In the olden days, whale bones were used to make corsets for women and men. These corsets would squash in a person's body so that he or she looked slimmer.

What makes my joints pop?

The popping bubbles in your joints make that sound! The joints on your body are where the bones meet. A thick liquid called synovial fluid surrounds your joints to keep them lubricated. Sometimes gases are pushed in the synovial fluid. When you stretch your joints far enough, gas bubbles pop and produce the popping sound that you hear.

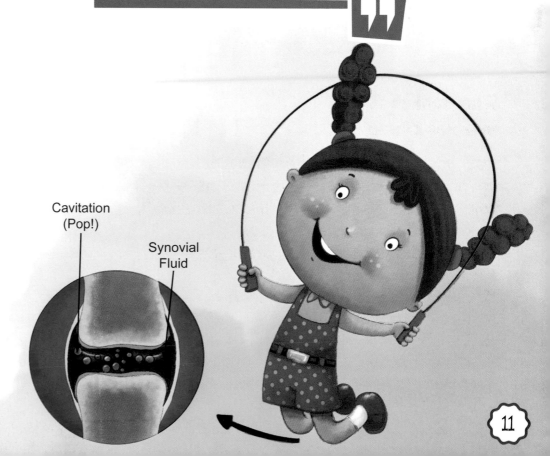

Cavitation (Pop!)

Synovial Fluid

What is inside my brain?

Your brain contains millions of nerve cells. These cells are grey, white and pink (a few of them) in colour and have texture like tofu! They are connected end-to-end and come together to make up the brain, vertebral column and the nervous system.

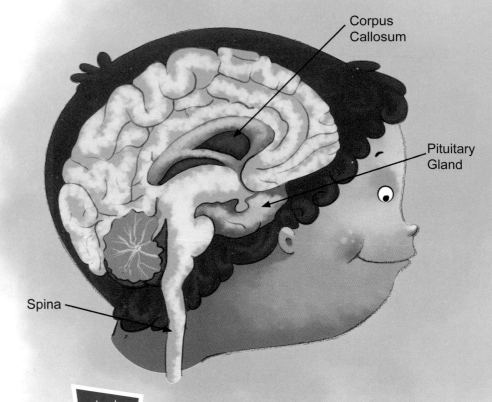

Corpus Callosum

Pituitary Gland

Spina

Find out

Have you heard about ice cream headaches? Why do we get them?

Pocket fact

The cerebrum (largest part of the brain) is divided into two halves. The left half controls the right side of the body and the right half controls the left side.

What is a headache?

Headache is not actually caused by pain in your brain. In reality, your brain can only tell you when other parts of your body hurt but can't actually feel pain. Sometimes the muscles or blood vessels that cover your head swell and become larger, causing pain. The surrounding nerves immediately send a rush of messages to your brain, and that is when you get a headache.

What do I have a belly button for?

Your belly button is the spot where your umbilical cord was once attached. The umbilical cord carries oxygen and nutrients from the mother to the foetus inside the womb. But once a baby is born, it doesn't need an umbilical cord. The doctor cuts the cord and a tiny stump is left. When this stump falls off after a few weeks, you are left with a belly button.

Find out

How long does it take for food to reach your stomach?

Pocket fact

Acid in the stomach!
Your stomach contains hydrochloric acid which helps in digestion and kills bacteria and viruses that may enter the body along with the food you eat.

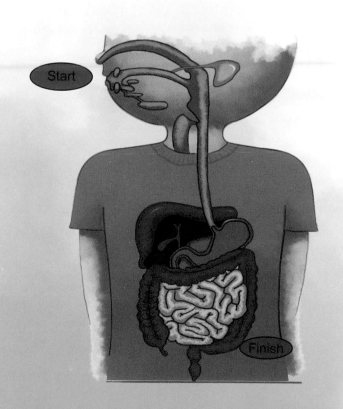

Start

Finish

What happens when food goes inside my body?

The food you eat gets digested. Food is broken down into simple substances (glucose, glycerine etc) in your body. This process is known as digestion. Digestion takes place in two different parts: the stomach and small intestine. Your stomach releases juices and churns food. These juices turn large food particles into smaller ones, which are absorbed in the blood.

What is locked inside my rib cage?

Your heart and lungs are the important organs that the rib cage protects. Lungs help you in respiration and the heart pumps blood into your body. Your ribs act as bodyguards, protecting your heart and lungs. If you didn't have ribs, these organs would be in danger every time you walk down the street or play sports!

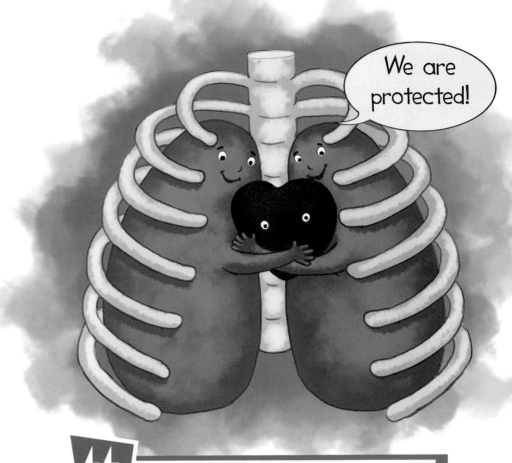

We are protected!

Find out

What is a stethoscope used for?

Pocket fact

Your heart pumps about 100 gallons of blood through the body each hour—enough to fill 1,600 drinking glasses.

What makes my heart go 'lub-dub'?

The 'lub-dub' of your heart is the sound of your heart beat! Your heart does the important job of pumping blood and oxygen throughout the body. There are tubes that carry blood and oxygen around your body from the heart. The sound of your heart beat is made by these tubes as they open and close to pump blood in and out.

What are tonsils and tonsillitis?

Tonsils are lumps of tissue located at the back of your throat on both sides. They help fight infections. Tonsillitis happens when your tonsils become infected by bacteria or viruses. Your tonsils may become red and swollen, or have a white or yellow coating on them.

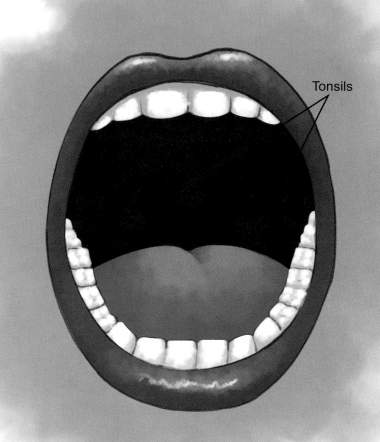

Tonsils

 Find out

The pharynx at the back of your nose and mouth carries both air and food. Then why doesn't food enter your windpipe?

 Pocket fact

Ear! Nose! Throat!
A doctor who takes care of all these parts is called an otolaryngologist (also called an ENT doctor).

What is the Adam's apple?

It's another name for your voice box or larynx. Your larynx grows larger in your teens and sticks out from your throat. This is called the Adam's apple. Everyone's larynx grows during their teens, but larynx in girls doesn't grow as much as it does in boys. That's why only boys have Adam's apple!

Index